The Holy Spirit

John Paul

A Doctrinal Study

Cover design and art work: John T. Paul

ISBN-13: 978-0-9884032-2-2

ISBN-10: 0-9884032-2-6

Library of Congress Catalog Number: 2017902797

Printed in the United States of America

www.WordDrivenSpiritLed.com

CONTENTS

FOR

MY WIFE,

ANILA

AND MY

DAUGHTERS,

RHEMA

NASYA

NITA

NYSA

CHAPTER 1

INTRODUCTION

He hovered over the waters as God created the heavens and the earth. He empowered Gideon who choose just three hundred men and defeated the Mideanites. He descended as a dove on Jesus Christ when John baptized Him. He is the seven fold Spirit of God as described in Isaiah 11:2. Any blasphemy against Him will not be forgiven. He was there when I first accepted Jesus as my Savior, and He continues to work in my life as I make Jesus my Master. He is the Holy Spirit, the third person of the Trinity.

Let us see how and where the Holy Spirit, fits into the transformation process described in Romans 12:2. We will see how the Holy Spirit comes *alongside* to convict the sinner, and then *indwells* in the born-again believer and finally *fills* the believer. This is the three phased process involving the Holy Spirit as He transforms a sinner into a living sacrifice that is holy and acceptable to God.

> I beseech you therefore, brethren, by the mercies of God, that you present your bodies a living sacrifice, holy, acceptable to God, which is your reasonable service. And do not be conformed to this world, but be transformed by the renewing of your mind, that you may prove what is that good and acceptable and perfect will of God. (Romans 12:1-2)

Let me illustrate the role of the Holy Spirit using an age old tradition that has been followed in India. This is the tradition of matchmaking. For a fee, a marriage broker will bring 10 to 15 pictures of beautiful prospective brides to the groom's parents for their review. The relationship between Jesus Christ and the born-again Christian is described as a marriage in the Bible. Similar to a marriage broker for an earthly marriage, there is a marriage broker for the spiritual marriage that starts here on earth but continues on into heaven and into eternity. That spiritual marriage broker is the Holy Spirit himself. I call him the Celestial Marriage Broker.

To understand the role of the Holy Spirit in this spiritual marriage, we must first understand the nature of the marriage. The actual spiritual wedding does not take place until Christ returns. Revelation paints a picture of what happens at the wedding.

> Rev 19:6 And I heard, as it were, the voice of a great multitude, as the sound of many waters and as the sound of mighty thunderings, saying, "Alleluia! For the Lord God Omnipotent reigns! 7 Let us be glad and rejoice and give Him glory, for the marriage of the Lamb has come, and His wife has made herself ready." 8 And to her it was granted to be arrayed in fine linen, clean and bright, for the fine linen is the righteous acts of the saints.

There are few important things that we need to clearly understand here. First, we read that the marriage of the Lamb has come. This means that today the church, being the bride of the Lamb, is still getting ready to meet the Lamb, Jesus Christ, who is the groom. Second, we see that the bride has made herself ready. During this waiting period, from the time the bride was introduced to Jesus Christ (at the point of salvation) to the time she meets Jesus face to face for the actual wedding, she has been carefully preparing herself. Third, we see that the bride was given fine linen representing the righteousness of the bride. The bride here is none other than the church.

To better understand the entire meaning of this scripture, let me give a brief description of the Jewish wedding process.

The very first step in a Jewish wedding is the matchmaking process. The groom's father calls a *Shadchan,* the match-maker, to select a bride for his son. Once that selection is completed and both sets of parents agree on the match, a betrothal is then planned. The betrothal is a ceremony where a marriage covenant is established between the bride and the groom. This is similar to an engagement in today's culture, except that it cannot be broken. During the betrothal ceremony, the groom places a betrothal ring on the bride's finger. This ring signifies a seal or a reminder to the bride and everyone else that the bride is already spoken for and that the bridegroom will come back for his bride after a certain period of time. As part of the betrothal, the bridegroom negotiates the price (mohar) with the bride's father. This is the price he will pay to purchase his bride. Nullifying the betrothal is equivalent to a divorce. As a symbol of this agreement, the bride and groom drink from a cup of wine that has been blessed. The bridegroom then leaves the bride in her father's house and returns to his father's house where he proceeds to prepare a place for his bride. During this time, the bride carefully prepares herself, waiting for the expected return of her husband to take her back to his father's house and consummate the marriage. Interestingly, it is the groom's father who determines when his son is ready to go bring his bride to live with them.

You might already have seen the similarities between the Jewish wedding and the spiritual wedding between the church and our Lord Jesus Christ. Let me focus on the spiritual *Shadchan*, the Celestial Marriage Broker. He brokers the marriage covenant between the individuals that make up the church and the Lord Jesus Christ. He does this based on His intimate knowledge of both parties involved.

Let us start with the first introduction between the sinner and the savior. Have you ever heard your friend or someone say "He got saved because of me?" We need to be very careful about such statements as we are taking credit for something we did not do. No human being has the power to convert a person or make a person believe in Jesus Christ. When we share the gospel, we bear witness to what Christ has done in our own lives. The actual conviction is accomplished by the Holy Spirit. He, because of his intimate knowledge of the condition of the sinner's heart and the unconditional love of Jesus Christ, has the power to convict a sinner of his or her need for the Savior.

> John 16:8 And when He has come, He will convict the world of sin, and of righteousness, and of judgment: 9 of sin, because they do not believe in Me;

> 1 Cor 12:3 Therefore I make known to you that no one speaking by the Spirit of God calls Jesus accursed, and no one can say that Jesus is Lord except by the Holy Spirit.

The Holy Spirit comes ***alongside*** the sinner and introduces the sinner to the Savior. But you may say that you don't see or feel his presence at salvation. A good way to explain that is using the concept of floodlighting a building or monument or an architectural structure. When an engineer looks to lighting up a building, there are two requirements. One is that the building's form, beauty and architectural identity is not disturbed or obscured. The second is that the building should be illuminated to a level that reveals its texture and the character of the architectural design. The trick to doing this is to hide the floodlights so that they are not seen nor do they obscure the view of the building. That is how the Holy Spirit works. He is right there, but the focus is not on him, the marriage broker, but on the groom, Jesus Christ. He never says, "Look at me, I am the one who made this happen." Rather, He says, "Look at Jesus, your groom, your future husband; trust in Him; love him." The Holy Spirit is the hidden floodlight illuminating Jesus Christ and His character so we may see every detail of His beauty and His love, and fall in love with Him. This is the first task of the celestial marriage broker – coming alongside to introduce the sinner to the savior.

When a person meets Jesus Christ for the first time, unknown to us, a betrothal celebration takes place. At this time of salvation, as the person (the bride) is betrothed to Jesus Christ (the groom), the angels in heaven are celebrating this betrothal.

> Luke 15:10 Likewise, I say to you, there is joy in the presence of the angels of God over one sinner who repents.

While the angels are celebrating, the groom, Jesus Christ, is confirming His commitment to the bride by placing a *ring* as a sign or seal of His return. This seal is the Holy Spirit.

> Eph 1:13 In Him you also trusted, after you heard the word of truth, the gospel of your salvation; in whom also, having believed, you were sealed with the Holy Spirit of promise, 14 who is the guarantee of our inheritance until the redemption of the purchased possession, to the praise of His glory.

Unlike the marriage brokers of the world whose job is done with the betrothal, this celestial marriage broker, the Holy Spirit, continues to stay with the bride to help her prepare for the groom's return.

> John 16:13 However, when He, the Spirit of truth, has come, He will guide you into all truth; for He will not speak on His own authority, but whatever He hears He will speak; and He will tell you things to come. 14 He will glorify Me, for He will take of what is Mine and declare it to you. 15 All things that the Father has are Mine. Therefore I said that He will take of Mine and declare it to you.

Let us examine the above scripture. There are four subjects in it. The main subject is obviously the Holy Spirit referred to as "He" nine times. Then there is "you," meaning every born-again Christian that makes up the bride of Christ. Next there is "Me," referring to Jesus Christ himself, and finally there is the Father. Herein are all the ingredients required to prepare the bride for Christ's return. Not only is the Holy Spirit the marriage broker, He now transitions to be a permanent marriage counselor who continues to illuminate Jesus Christ and teaches the bride (you and me) everything we need to learn about our future husband, Jesus Christ. He does this now by ***indwelling*** in us as the seal of Jesus' commitment to come back for us.

> 1 Cor 3:16 Do you not know that you are the temple of God and that the Spirit of God dwells in you?

> John 14:26 But the Helper [counselor, NIV], the Holy Spirit, whom the Father will send in My name, He will teach you all things, and bring to your remembrance all things that I said to you.

The above scripture is significant for us as we learn to understand how the Holy Spirit affects the transformation in our lives. He does this from the inside out, not from the outside in. From a human standpoint, change is normally affected by controlling the behavior, which is from the outside. From a spiritual standpoint, change has to be affected by changing the heart, which is from the inside. All through the preparation period, from the time a sinner is born-again to the time Christ returns, the Holy Spirit is slowly working on the condition of the heart.

When I first met Jesus Christ, I wanted to please him so much. I tried to stop doing what I knew was wrong and tried to do what I knew was right. But I had the same dilemma as Paul.

> Rom 7:15 For what I am doing, I do not understand. For what I will to do, that I do not practice; but what I hate, that I do.

This dilemma can only be overcome when the Holy Spirit ***fills*** the believer. It wasn't until I figured out what it meant to be filled with the Holy Spirit, that I started seeing changes in my heart. We will study this concept in Chapter 16.

If we allow him to, He, the marriage counselor, will teach us, train us, clean house (the heart) and prepare us for Christ's return.

The Holy Spirit, the celestial marriage broker, came ***alongside*** and introduced us to Jesus Christ. When we accepted Jesus Christ as our savior, He began to ***indwell*** in us and became our permanent life counselor. Now let Him ***fill*** us with His power and teach us to get ready for the beautiful wedding waiting for us. We must not only learn to recognize the presence and counsel of the Holy Spirit, but also learn to submit to His direction.

To be led by the Holy Spirit we must understand the Holy Spirit Power required for this incredible and supernatural transformation from a sinful life to a holy life. But this transformation is not perfected overnight. Rather, it is a progressive holiness realized over time as the believer prepares his or her heart for the spiritual wedding to come.

In the next few chapters we will examine the Baptism and Filling of the Holy Spirit through -

1) The Authority of God's Word

2) The Prominence of God's Word

3) The Sufficiency of Christ

4) The Nature of God

5) Dealing with Difficult Scripture

6)   Speaking in tongues

7)   Names & Titles of the Holy Spirit

8)   The Power of the Holy Spirit

It is through one these avenues that heresy, division, or misunderstanding have traditionally entered Christian circles. Our study will approach the subject not only to be informative, but to protect the student (you) from pitfalls he/she may encounter in the future.

To understand the doctrine of the Baptism and Filling of the Holy Spirit we must first establish the authority of the Word of God. Both the doctrines held by Charismatic and Pentecostal movements concerning the Holy Spirit and the interpretation of gifts strike at the heart of the authority of God's Word. We will, therefore, first approach this argument from two angles – the authority which God gives His Word and the prominence of the Word of God. Once we have established this foundation, we will address the remaining doctrinal areas.

CHAPTER 1

PERSONAL

NOTES

CHAPTER 2

THE AUTHORITY

GOD GIVES

HIS WORD

PRINCIPLE #1

Answer the questions first and then fill in the principle in the space provided.

Principle #1:_____

_____

_____

a)   II Corinthians 5:7 – Key Thought: _____

_____

1) The verse begins with the word "for". It should cause us to think "For what?" or "Because of what?". Read the preceding six verses and then write a one-sentence summary of them.

2) Who does the "we" speak to in verse 7?

3) What does the word "walk" mean?

4) Explain the difference between walking by faith and walking by sight.

5) Read Hebrews 11:8-10

i)   How would this be an example of walking by faith and not by sight?

ii)   What would be the application to the disciple (you) and the Word?

b)   Galatians 1:6-12 – Key Thought: _____

_____

1)   What is the problem Paul faces in this verse?

2)   What two hypothetical characters are presented as potential bearers of false doctrine?

i) _____

ii) _____

3) Specifically, how does Paul express his feelings towards bearers of false doctrine?

    i) _____

    ii) _____

    iii) _____

4) Paul disclaims two ways of receiving doctrines. What are they, and why is it important to Paul that they were not used?

    i) _____

    _____

    ii) _____

    _____

5) We have both classes which lack authority and which carry authority. Fill in the blanks below:

    Lacks authority:

    Has authority:

c) From the two passages, what does God's Word take precedence over? (list these things)

d) Write in Principle #1 in the space provided at the beginning of this section.

PRINCIPLE #2

Answer the questions first and then fill in the principle in the space provided.

Principle #2:_____

_____

_____

_____

a) From the passages below, draw a principle that has to do with the authority of God's Word.

Verse   Principle

John 1:1, 14   _____

II Timothy 3:16_____

Hebrews 4:12,13_____

II Peter 1:20,21 _____

What unifying theme links these four passages?

b) From the verses below, come up with a unifying theme or principle.

Exodus 4:22; Joshua 24:2; II Samuel 7:5; I kings 12:24; I Chronicles 17:4; Isaiah 10:24; Jeremiah 2:2; Ezekiel 3:11; Amos 2:1; Obadiah 1:1; Micah 2:3; Nahum 1:12; Zechariah 1:3

What is God trying to tell us about the authorship of the Bible?

c) Write in the principle #2 in the space provided at the beginning of this section.

PRINCIPLE #3

Answer the questions first and then fill in the principle in the space provided.

Principle #3:_____

_____

_____

_____

a) The following passages each speak to a function or use of God's Word in our everyday lives. Read the verses and fill in the blanks as they pertain to the function of God's Word in our lives.

Verse   Principle

Psalm 119:9,11_____

Psalm 119:105_____

John 17:17_____

II Timothy 2:15_____

II Timothy 3:17_____

b) How do these passages speak to the authority of God's Word?

c) Write in the principle #3 in the space provided at the beginning of this section.

Which of these three principles have you been most susceptible to violate? Explain.

CONCLUSION

Cross reference these two statement with Scripture.

1. God's Word will take precedence over all experience, both personal and otherwise.

2. No matter what we observe, personally sense or feel, it will be judged true of false strictly on the bases of God's Word.

CHAPTER 2

PERSONAL

NOTES

CHAPTER 3

THE PROMINENCE

OF THE

WORD OF GOD

This brings us to the second major issue in establishing God's Word as authoritative. The first was from a positive angle, that being the authority that God gives His Word. The second is from a negative angle, and is based more on need, especially when dealing with the Holy Spirit. In God's three manifestations of His person, Satan is more at home here – the spiritual realm. Satan's impersonations of God the Father prove impotent rather than omnipotent. Satan's impersonations of God the Son quickly reveal themselves as sinful shams, but it is the spiritual realm in which Satan lives and in which he feels most at home.

PRINCIPLE #1

Answer the questions first and then fill in the principle in the space provided.

Principle #1:_____

_____

_____

_____

Read the passages, write in the key thoughts as they pertain to this subject.

Ephesians 6:10_____

Ephesians 6:11_____

_____

Ephesians 6:12_____

_____

Acts 26:18_____

_____

a) From the preceding passages:
   1) What has Satan established?

   2) What does he have at his disposal?

b) Write in Principle #1 in the space provided at the beginning of this section.

PRINCIPLE #2

Answer the questions first and then fill in the principle in the space provided.

Principle #2:_____

_____

_____

_____

Read the passages, write in the key thoughts as they pertain to this subject.

II Corinthians 11:13_____

II Corinthians 11:14_____

II Corinthians 11:15_____

Job 1:6_____

a) What does the fact that Satan was able to make himself at home among the angels and the throne of God tell us?

b) What is the significance of Satan disguising himself as an angel of light? What is this?

c) Who are his servants in verse 15?

d) What is their ability and how does this affect us?

e) Write in Principle #2 in the space provided at the beginning of this section.

PRINCIPLE #3

Answer the questions first and then fill in the principle in the space provided.

Principle #3:_____

_____

_____

Read the passages, write in the key thoughts as they pertain to this subject.

Exodus 7:11-13, 22-23_____

_____

Job 1:12-19_____

_____

Job 2:6-8_____

_____

Psalm 106:37_____

_____

Mark 5:6,7_____

_____

Luke 4:5,6_____

_____

Luke 4:9-11_____

_____

Revelation 12:9_____

_____

Revelation 13:11-17_____

_____

Revelation 20:7-10_____

_____

a) List any questions you have about the passages you have just read.

b) Break the 10 passages up into several broad headings and list them with corresponding verses.

c) Write in Principle #3 in the space provided at the beginning of this section.

Below is a hypothetical situation for spiritual deception. As you read the paragraph, you will notice at each point of deception there is a number. Below the paragraph there are corresponding numbers with accompanying spaces. In the spaces write the proof scripture and key thought from the above study and the related proof scripture that establishes this as a viable illustration of Satan attempting to deceive. All of the scriptures in this chapter are available as proof scripture.

a)   SITUATION – You are sitting in your room late at night reading. All is dark except for a light glow from your bedside lamp. You are all alone. As you look up you notice that a blaze of fiery white light is showing through the cracks of your closed bedroom door, It is of such intensity that it frames the door and permeates the room. Suddenly the door flies open with a roar which prostrates you in your room. The room is flooded with a shining 1) white light which your eyes can hardly endure. Before you stands a giant 2) angelic creature and with a strange roar he speaks. Although the sound is suffocating, you can still comprehend his words. "My name is Michael and I stand in the presence of God. I have come to give you a new 3) teaching. You shall bring a new revelation to man and you shall be my 4) prophet." You ask him for a sign as a fleece, and you are astonished as 5) he gives you miraculous powers and as 6) he breathes life into the ceramic figures on your desk. You challenge him and he 7) proclaims Jesus as the "Holy One of God" and "Son of the Most High God". He then gives you the sign of prophet Elijah, 8) he calls down fire from heaven and 9) shows you extensive passages from the Bible to prove a second coming of Elijah before Christ. 10) He then gives you prophetic utterances – all of which come true and 11) he gives you the ability to give life to a statue. 12) You are his prophet and the 13) nations follow you.

1) _____

_____

2) _____

_____

3) _____

_____

4) _____

_____

5) _____

_____

6) _____

_____

7) _____

_____

8) _____

_____

9) _____

_____

10) _____

_____

11) _____

_____

12) _____

_____

13) _____

_____

b) What have you as a Christian been deceived into doing?

c) Is this deception plausible for the average Christian? Why?

Which of these three principles have you been most susceptible to violating? Explain.

SUMMARY

1) God's Word will take precedence over all experiences, both personal and otherwise.
2) No matter what we observe, personally sense or feel, it will be judged true or false strictly on the basis of God's Word.
3) If it is true to God's Word, even though we don't experience it, it will still be judged by us to be true.
4) If it is in contradiction to God's Word, even if we do experience it, it will be judged to be false and not of God.

CHAPTER 3

PERSONAL

NOTES

CHAPTER 4

THE SUFFICIENCY

OF

JESUS CHRIST

At this point in the study we must look at the doctrinal teachings of the Holy Spirit as they relate to the theme of the Sufficiency of Christ. False doctrines on this subject strike at the heart of the doctrine of the Sufficiency of Christ. It is mere semantics to say that Christ is sufficient, because He provides access to the Holy Spirit. Unless Christ truly provides all, then Christ is not sufficient. For Christ to be sufficient He must provide all, not merely provide a springboard to that second experience which provides all. If you can have Christ and yet not have access to the Holy Spirit without a second experience, then Christ is not sufficient because more is needed. These doctrines then sound of heresy, for the sufficiency of Christ is the key cornerstone of the church and of discipleship.

PRINCIPLE #1

Answer the questions first and then fill in the principle in the space provided.

Principle #1:_____

_____

_____

_____

Read the passages, write in the key thoughts as they pertain to this subject.

Matthew 28:19,20_____

_____

John 7:32-39_____

_____

Romans 8:9_____

_____

Romans 8:14,15_____

_____

Titus 3:5_____

_____

I Corinthians 12:13_____

_____

II Corinthians 1:21,22_____

_____

Ephesians 1:13,14_____

_____

I Peter 1:1-5_____

_____

I John 3:24_____

_____

PRINCIPLE #2

Answer the questions first and then fill in the principle in the space provided.

Principle #2:_____

_____

_____

_____

Read the passages, write in the key thoughts as they pertain to this subject.

John 16:7,13-15_____

_____

II Corinthians 1:17-20_____

_____

Ephesians 1:3_____

_____

Colossians 1:18,19_____

_____

Colossians 2:9_____

_____

II Peter 1:2,3_____

_____

II Peter 1:4_____

_____

PRINCIPLE #3

Answer the questions first and then fill in the principle in the space provided.

Principle #3:_____

_____

_____

Read the passages, write in the key thoughts as they pertain to this subject.

John 16:14_____

_____

I Timothy 2:5,6_____

_____

SUMMARY

Using proof texts, verify the following statements by placing the appropriate passages in the blank which follows each statement to be proven.

A.   We have the Holy Spirit _____ at the

point of salvation _____ as a result of the total

sufficiency of Christ. _____

B.   We have all spiritual blessings _____, God's

fullness _____, all spiritual needs pertaining to life and

godliness _____ and in fact all that God has to

offer _____ as a result of the total sufficiency of

Christ. _____

C.   We have need of no other work of grace to draw us closer to

God _____ or supply us with additional spiritual

tools _____ as a result of the sufficiency of Christ.

_____

D.   In your own words, write out a simple statement which you
feel sums up the doctrine of the Sufficiency of Christ as it pertains
to the Holy Spirit.

CHAPTER 4

PERSONAL

NOTES

CHAPTER 5

THE NATURE

OF

GOD – PART I

At this point in the study we must look at the doctrinal teachings of the nature of God as it pertains to the Holy Spirit. The doctrines of the Charismatic/Pentecostal movements concerning the Holy Spirit and the Nature of God are not just varying shades of gray on obscure theological issues, but rather strike at the heart of Biblical orthodoxy. They do so without pronouncement or teaching because they are based upon experiences, experiences interpreted into doctrine, the truth of which is based on the undeniable occurrence and results of experiences rather than on the infallible Word of God. To accept this doctrine by default or by experience is to deviate from the Nature of God as presented by the Word of God.

PRINCIPLE #1

Answer the questions first and then fill in the principle in the space provided.

Principle #1:_____

_____

_____

_____

Read the passages, write in the key thoughts as they pertain to this subject.

Deuteronomy 6:4_____

_____

John 1:1-3,16_____

_____

John 4:24_____

_____

John 10:38_____

_____

John 14:9-11_____

_____

I Corinthians 8:4_____

_____

II Corinthians 5:19_____

_____

Ephesians 4:4-6_____

_____

Colossians 2:9_____

_____

<u>Consider these definitions of unity</u>

Thiesan; Lecture in Systemic Theology, page 134; "By unity of God, we mean that there is one God (Deut 6:4) and that the divine nature is undivided and indivisible (John 10:30, Gal 4:6). This unity, however, is not inconsistent with the Trinity (Eph 4:4-6), for a unity is not the same as a unit."

Berkhof; Systemic Theology, page 62; "We use the term unity to describe the state or quality of being simple, the condition of being free from division into parts, and therefore from composition (I John 5:7,8)......It means that God is not a composite (I Cor 8:4) and is not susceptible to division in any sense of the word (John 10:38, I John 5:6,7).

PRINCIPLE #2

Answer the questions first and then fill in the principle in the space provided.

Principle #2:_____

_____

_____

_____

Read the passages, write in the key thoughts as they pertain to this subject.

Matthew 3:16,17_____

_____

Matthew 28:19, 20_____

_____

Acts 20:28_____

_____

II Corinthians 13:14_____

Ephesians 2:18_____

I Thessalonians 1:2-5_____

II Thessalonians 2:13-16_____

I Peter 1:2_____

I John 5:7_____

Revelation 1:6-10_____

SUMMARY

Watson, Institutes, I, 474 Atanasian Creed "We worship one God in Trinity (John10:30/Matt 3:16,17/2 Cor 5:19/Gal 4:6) and trinity in Unity (I John3:7,8); neither confounding the persons nor dividing the substance, for there is one person of the Father (John 10:29), another of the son (Matt 3:17) and another of the Holy Spirit (Mark 1:10/John 1:32), but the Godhead of the Father, the son, and of the Holy Ghost is all one (John 10:30/II Cor 3:17,18), the glory equal (Phil 2:6), the majesty coeternal. So the Father is God (John 5:18), the Son is God (John 1:1) and the Holy Ghost is God (II Cor 3:17); and yet there are not three Gods, but one God (Deut 6:4).

CHAPTER 5

PERSONAL

NOTES

CHAPTER 6

THE NATURE

OF

GOD – PART II

At this point in the study we must look at the doctrinal teachings of the nature of God as it pertains to the Trinity. Each principle in this chapter refers to a specific function of a member of the Godhead.

PRINCIPLE #1: GOD THE _____

Answer the questions first and then fill in the principle in the space provided.

Read the passages, write in the key thoughts as they pertain to this subject.

Ephesians 1:20_____

_____

Colossians 1:17_____

_____

Colossians 1:27_____

_____

Colossians 3:3_____

_____

Hebrews 7:25_____

_____

Hebrews 8:1,2_____

_____

Revelation 3:20_____

_____

PRINCIPLE #2: GOD THE _____

Read the passages, write in the key thoughts as they pertain to this subject.

John 16:7,8_____

_____

Romans 8:26,27_____

_____

I Corinthians 12:4-7_____

_____

Galatians 5:22_____

_____

Ephesians 1:13_____

_____

Ephesians 4:30_____

_____

I John 2:27_____

_____

PRINCIPLE #3: GOD THE _____

Read the passages, write in the key thoughts as they pertain to this subject.

Job 1:6_____

_____

Jeremiah 23:23,24_____

_____

John 17:15_____

_____

John 17:17_____

_____

Ephesians 2:4-6_____

_____

Colossians 3:3_____

_____

Revelation 7:10_____

_____

PRINCIPLE #4: GOD THE _____

Read the passages, write in the key thoughts as they pertain to this subject.

Genesis 1:1_____

_____

Genesis 1:2_____

_____

Psalm 104:30_____

_____

Ephesians 3:9_____

_____

Colossians 1:15-16_____

_____

Genesis 1:26_____

_____

Genesis 11:7_____

_____

John 14:23_____

_____

I Corinthians 3:16_____

I Corinthians 6:16-18_____

I Corinthians 6:19_____

Leviticus 20:8_____

John 10:36_____

Romans 15:16_____

I Corinthians 1:2_____

Jeremiah 44:4,5_____

John 16:7,8_____

SUMMARY

A.   From the study of the Nature of God up to this point, chose proof tests to support the statement of Augustine as written below. Write the appropriate proof text in the blank following the statement concerning the Nature of God.

"All those catholic expounders of the divine Scriptures whom I have been able to read, who have written before me concerning the Trinity, who is God _____, have purposed to teach, according to the Scriptures, this doctrine, that the Father_____, and the Son _____ and the Holy Spirit _____, intimate a divine unity _____ of one and the same substance in an indivisible equality _____ and, therefore, that these are not three Gods, but one God_____.

B. Reconcile these two verses – Deut 6:4 and Matt 28:19, 20

CHAPTER 6

PERSONAL

NOTES

CHAPTER 7

THE NATURE

OF

GOD – PART III

At this point in the study we must look at the doctrinal teachings of the nature of God as it pertains to the equality of the members of the Trinity. There are some false doctrines and philosophies that separate the work of the Holy Spirit from that of the Son. There are some that elevate the work of the Holy Spirit above the work of the Son. We will examine the Word of God extensively to determine the separation (or the lack of) between the members of the Trinity.

Consider the following beliefs of some major churches.

The following is a direct quote from The Assemblies of God's Statement of Fundamental Truths. Link is provided below followed by their belief on the baptism of the Holy Spirit (copied and pasted from their website on Jan 19, 2017).

http://ag.org/top/Beliefs/Statement_of_Fundamental_Truths/sft_short.cfm

"WE BELIEVE...**the Baptism in the Holy Spirit is a Special Experience Following Salvation** that empowers believers for witnessing and effective service, just as it did in New Testament times. [1 of 4 cardinal doctrines of the AG]"

The following is a direct quote from The Pentecostal Church of God's beliefs. Link is provided below followed by their belief on the baptism of the Holy Spirit (copied and pasted from their website on Jan 19, 2017).

http://www.pcg.org/beliefs

"8. The Baptism of the Holy Ghost

The Baptism of the Holy Ghost and fire (Matthew 3:11), is a gift from God, as promised by the Lord Jesus Christ to all believers in this dispensation of time, and is received subsequent to the new birth (John 14:16, 17; Acts 1:8; 2:38, 39; 10:44-48). The Baptism of the Holy Ghost is accompanied by speaking in other tongues as the Holy Spirit Himself gives utterance as the initial physical sign and evidence (Acts 2:4)."

As you read the above statements, you begin to see that one must have a special experience to be baptized by the Holy Spirit which must then be accompanied by speaking in tongues. This presents a doctrine that the Holy Spirit does something separately and without cooperation from other members of the Trinity. Let's look at the scripture to determine if there is actually a separation of the Holy Spirit from the other members of the Trinity

1. Consider -

    a) The individual is saved by the indwelling of Jesus Christ, but he does not experience the work of the Holy Spirit.

    b) There is a second work of grace on the part of the Holy Spirit in the life of the believer, a definite point in time that can be referred back to as the baptism of the Holy Spirit.

At this point, the believer has experienced the work of Jesus Christ by being saved and the work of the Holy Spirit by being empowered for sanctification and ministry. What must the believer yet experience to complete his experience of the Godhead in its totality?

2.   Explain the error of this type of thinking.

3.   Each of the scriptures below describe a type of relationship
     with a member of the Godhead. Next to each verse, specify
     the member spoken of and describe the relationship.

Scripture	Member of Godhead	Relationship Described
Exodus 20:1-5		
Luke 9:23		
Galatians 2:20		
Galatians 5:16		
Ephesians 5:18		
I Peter 1:15,16		

From the table above, would it be possible to have the
relationships described with any one member of the Godhead

without having an equal and reciprocal relationship with the other two as well? Develop fully the answer to this questions. Supply proof texts.

4. In dealing with the separation of the Holy Spirit from other members of the Godhead, we find that certain terms and watchwords take on a mystical, almost magical form in the person's relationship with God. Thus, unless the person knows the correct words or terms to use in praying to God, his prayers are unanswered irrespective of the heart or of the previous work of grace as accomplished by Christ.

An illustration of God hearing the intent of man's heart when he doesn't know the words or fully understand the process is seen in Luke 7:36-50.

a) Who are the characters in this narrative?

b) Which of these characters did Christ seek?

c) Which characters verbally invited Christ to be with them?

d) Were they seeking Christ (verbally)?

e) Which characters did not verbally invite Christ?

f) Was she seeking Christ (verbally)?

g) What did the woman ask Christ to do for her?

h) What did Christ do for her?

i) When she became a Christian, what prayer did she verbalize?

j) From this, what can we conclude that Christ heard and responded to if not her words?

5) In the same vein, lets take as an example a hypothetical individual who has been praying and seeking the Lordship of Christ as described in Galatians 2:20. Read Galatians 2:20 and paraphrase it below in the way it would be prayed to God.

a) Could Christ answer this prayer without controlling and filling the person with the Holy Spirit as described in Ephesians 5:18?

b) Would God ignore these prayers? Why or why not?

6) In summarizing both of these cases, it will be of great aid to:

a) Instruct the prostitute in Luke 7 (now converted) in the correct doctrines of salvation so that she may share her faith more effectively.

b) Instruct the fervent saint who is praying in Galatians 2:20 on the fact that God the Father must also be submitted to and that God the Holy Spirit must also have control of our lives., This, of course, is done so that the individual may fully understand the functional correlation between the members of the Trinity as they work in the life of the believer. This will help him cooperate and aid him in helping others. We must not assume, however, that since an individual lacks theological sophistication that he or she cannot experience salvation or the work of the Holy Spirit.

c) Write a summary statement depicting the separate role of the Holy Spirit from the other members of the Godhead in the lives of believers as proposed by the Pentecostal and AOG churches.

d) Write the correct doctrinal position based upon your study of God's Word.

CHAPTER 7

PERSONAL

NOTES

CHAPTER 8

THE NATURE

OF

GOD – PART IV

At this point in the study we must look at the doctrinal teachings of the nature of God as it pertains to the third member of the Godhead, God the Holy Spirit, and His elevation above that of God the Father and God the Son.

1. There is a natural attraction to God and allurement of the supernatural and the spectacular. For most Christians, God the Father is perceived as demanding, strict, and a little dull, much like a corporate head, judge, or politician. God the Son is seen as nice; but, since you are going to heaven His work is finished. The mysterious God the Holy Spirit, on the other hand, with His miracles and gifts, holds a real attraction. This, of course, is a false conception of both the nature and the roles of the Godhead. It is always dangerous to single out any member of the Trinity for over-emphasis. According to John 16:13-15, why is this especially true of God the Holy Spirit?

2. According to the following verses, what is our devotional relationship with the members of the Godhead?

Scripture	Member of Godhead	Devotional Relationship
Psalm 70:4		
Psalm 150:1-6		
Luke 1:46, 47		
John 8:54-56		
Acts 19:17		
Philippians 2:9-11		
Colossians 1:3		
I Peter 1:3		

Which person of the Godhead is conspicuously absent from the these passages?

It must be determined whether or not there is any precedence for the praise and worship of the third member of the Godhead. To aid us in this, we will first look for examples.

3. Praise is an integral part of the opening of most of the Epistles. The following is a chart which be used to ascertain who is

praised in these openings.

Opening prayer of Epistles	Object of prayer or thanksgiving
Romans 1:8	
I Corinthians 1:4	
II Corinthians 1:3	
Galatians 1:3-5	
Ephesians 1:3	
Philippians 1:3	
Colossians 1:3	
I Thessalonians 1:2	
II Thessalonians 1:3	
II Timothy 1:3	
Philemon 4	
I Peter 1:3	

4. Praise is also an integral part of the closing benediction in the Epistles. The following chart will clearly show who is praised in these benedictions.

Closing benediction of Epistles	Object of prayer or thanksgiving
Romans 16:27	
Philippians 4:20	
II Timothy 4:18	
Hebrews 13:20,21	
I Peter 5:11	
II Peter 3:18	
Jude 1:25	

5. Since Acts is a classic book for illustrating the baptism, filling, and general work of the Holy Spirit, one would expect to find praise of these glorious works scattered throughout the book. Using an exhaustive concordance (online research), look up the word Spirit and Ghost in Acts. Record the number of times the Holy Spirit or Holy Ghost is praised in this book.

6. Within the Psalms are the classic prayers. You would expect to find repeated reference to the Holy Spirit as an object of praise. Following the same procedure as with Acts (online research), record the number of times the Holy Spirit or Holy Ghost is praised in the Psalms.

7. Follow this same procedure (online research) for each book of the Bible. How many times is the Holy Spirit praised in the Bible?

8. How often are we taught to praise Him?

9. Read Romans 8:1-25.

   a) List the work of Christ in this passage.

   b) List the work of the Holy Spirit in this passage.

c) How does this passage present the two as inseparable in function?

10. Read John 16:5-15

a) List the work of Christ in this passage.

b) List the work of the Holy Spirit in this passage.

c) How does this passage present the two as inseparable in function?

11. In the space below is summarized the basic reason that the philosophies of some churches/fellowships are deemed to be false. Next to each statement, supply a proof text that contradicts the teaching of these groups and then write the correct doctrinal statement.

    I) They separate the work of the Godhead from the other members of the Godhead.
    Proof text:
    Correct doctrinal statement:

    II) They create an almost cultic or mystical following around prayer to and for the Holy Spirit.
    Proof text:
    Correct doctrinal statement:

    III) They elevate the Holy Spirit above His rightful place in the Godhead.
    Proof text:
    Correct doctrinal statement:

    IV) They attribute praise to the Holy Spirit which is neither taught nor exemplified in Scripture.
    Proof text:
    Correct doctrinal statement:

CHAPTER 8

PERSONAL

NOTES

CHAPTER 9

DEALING WITH

DIFFICULT SCRIPTURE – PART I

There are some passages in the Bible that we do not understand completely. We need to be careful and not develop a doctrine to explain difficult scriptures.

1. The first step in understanding and dealing with difficult scripture (especially that which is seemingly contradictory) is to recognize the difference in types of Scripture. Scripture may be loosely grouped into three categories. For each group of scriptures below, give the passage a title and identify the type of scripture (narrative, symbolic, doctrinal).

Scripture type:

Passage	Title
Genesis 3:1-7	
Exodus 14:13-25	
Mark 1:9-11	
Acts 16:22-30	

Scripture type:

Passage	Title
II Samuel 12:1-4	
Daniel 8:1-15	
Luke 8:4-9	
Revelation 22:1-8	

Scripture type:

Passage	Title
Exodus 20:1-17	
Matthew 5:1-12	
Ephesians 5:22-6:9	
Hebrews 9:1-10:8	

From the above types – narrative, symbolic, doctrinal – only doctrine sets itself forward as the final authority of truth on a matter. Therefore, when studying a text, we should seek to understand its type and seek to isolate doctrinal teachings. Once doctrine has been isolated, two general rules can be followed.

2. Covenant Divisions – Doctrinal teachings are divided by the Old and New Covenants. When reading Scripture, it is important to interpret Old Covenant Doctrine in the light of any changes brought by the New Covenant.

    a) Read Leviticus 5:1-19. What is the doctrinal instruction here?

    b) Read Hebrews 9:1-10:18. What is the effect of these New Covenant teachings on the Old Covenant doctrine of guilt offering presented in Leviticus 5:1-19?

    c) What conclusion can be drawn about the relationship of Old Covenant doctrine to those of us in the New Covenant period?

3. Interpretation – Certain rules must also be followed which are based on the study up to this point.

    a) Doctrinal passages always interpret the other forms of Scripture.

    b) The other forms of Scripture may support doctrine, but they do not alter or interpret them.

c) Doctrinal Scripture itself must be able to stand alone as a clearly specific doctrinal teaching. It cannot be established clearly on the basis of symbols or narrative.

d) Read and title Luke 8:5-8

e) What type of Scripture is Luke 8:5-8?

f) Read and title Luke 8:9-15.

g) What type of Scripture is Luke 8:9-15?

h) Which interprets which? Why?

i) When reading Luke 8:5-8, in what way are our devotional insights and conclusions limited? Why?

4. In this same vein, how is prophetic Scripture limited in II Peter 1:20,21?

a) What light is similarly cast on the interpretation of historical narrative in Luke 24:27,44,45?

b) How does Deuteronomy 29:29 fit in with all of this?

5. Summarize your understanding of the types of Scripture and the limitations placed in using them to establish God's teaching on a subject.

6. Although errors from a misunderstanding of covenants do occur as well as from basing doctrine on symbols, by far the greatest frequency of error as it pertains to the Holy Spirit occurs from the tendency to create doctrinal teaching from narrative passages, or by the interpretation of doctrinal truth on the basis on narrative/historical events.

In the table below, read the passage and then give an example of erroneous doctrine which could be arrived at by the misuse of narrative Scripture

Passage	Erroneous Doctrine
Exodus 14:13-25	
II Kings 2:9-11	
John 11:1-46	
Acts 10:44-48	

What conclusions can you come to about the use of narrative Scripture for doctrinal purposes?

7. Closely linked to the issues involved with using narrative Scripture to establish doctrine is the issue of the Repeating Narrative Theme. Using the book of Acts, many argue that the historical references to the Holy Spirit are not simply narratives to be read individually, but instead they come together to form a theme in the book of such great strength that they should be accepted as doctrine. The fallacy of this argument is clear in that the Bible is full of repeating narrative themes. In the following tables, read the passage, title the event, give the repeating narrative theme, and create a corresponding doctrine (not a true doctrine).

Repeating Narrative Theme:

Passage	Event which takes place
Genesis 1:1,2,6,7	
Exodus 14:13-25	
Joshua 3:14-17	
II Kings 2:6-8	
II Kings 2:9-14	

(False) Doctrine:

Repeating Narrative Theme:

Passage	Event which takes place
Genesis 5:24	
II Kings 2:11,12	
Acts 1:9-11	

(False) Doctrine:

Repeating Narrative Theme:

Passage	Event which takes place
Exodus 2:15; 3:1	
I Samuel 23:14	
I Kings 19:1-8	
Luke 4:1,2	

(False) Doctrine:

8. What then are some of the dangers of using historical themes to establish doctrine?

9. Can you find any areas in your life that have been susceptible to the misuse of Scripture?

CHAPTER 9

PERSONAL

NOTES

CHAPTER 10

DEALING WITH

DIFFICULT SCRIPTURE – PART II

In this chapter we will look at the second step in understanding difficult Scripture, which is to recognize the limitations which Scripture places upon itself. The Bible clearly states that not all can or should be known by man. In the following tables below, read the key passage, record the key thought, give the limitation stated, and explain each example in the context of these limitations.

1. Key passage: Deuteronomy 29:29
   Key thought:

   Limitation:

Passage	Explanation
Before Genesis 1:1	
Time period covered in Luke 2:52	
John 21:25	
Acts 1:6,7	
Work of God between Malachi 4:6 and Matthew 1:1	

2. Key passage: Isaiah 55:8,9
   Key thought:

   Limitation:

Passage	Explanation
Matthew 13:10-17	
Matthew 16:8-12	
Hebrews 11:3	
II Peter 1:20,21	

3. Key passages: Daniel 9:7,14; Nehemiah 9:33; Romans 9:14-20
   Key thought:

   Limitation:

Passage	Explanation
Romans 9:15-29	
John 21:18-23	
Matthew 16:21-23	

4. Key passages: Revelation 22:18,19
    Key thought:

    Limitation:

Passage	Explanation
Acts 18:24-28	
Galatians 1:6-12	
II Thessalonians 2:1-12	
I Timothy 4:1-6	
II Timothy 2:16-19, 23	
II Timothy 4:3-5	
I John 4:1-6	
Revelation 13:13; 16:14; 19:20; 20:3; 20:10	

5. Summarize the limitations God places on us in our relationship with His Word.
    a.)

    b.)

c.)

d.)

6. What application does this have in the study of God's Word?

7. What application does this have in the teaching of God's Word?

8. God often tells us who, what, when, and where – He sometimes tells us how, but he often does not tell us why. In other words, God does not reveal His root motives. This is the same with many difficult scriptures. In the space below, give the Bible's explanation of this seeming mystery relying on the study you have just completed in this chapter.

9. Along the same line of thought, we may ask God "who", "what", "when", "how", "where". But we must never ask God "why" in such a way that brings into question His character. Explain this in the space provided below using Scripture to back up your explanation.

10. Review – List the types of Scripture.

11. Review – List the two primary divisions in the Bible which must be considered when reading doctrinal passages.

12. Review – List the rules which govern the supremacy of doctrine when establishing Biblical truth.
    a)

    b)

    c)

13. Review – Explain the fallacy of establishing doctrine with narrative passages.

14. Review – Explain the danger of establishing doctrine with repeating narrative themes.

15. Review – Explain how you would resolve as situation where you have a number of passages pointing to a clear doctrine development of a topic and there are a small number of historical and/or repeating passages which seem to contradict and/or you do not understand?

16. REMEMBER
    a) Only doctrine will substantiate the doctrine of the Holy Spirit.
    b) Only the New Covenant doctrines of the Holy Spirit will be irreversibly applicable.
    c) It is within reason to expect unexplainable revelations concerning the Holy Spirit.

17. ALWAYS INTERPRET SCRIPTURE IN LIGHT OF SCRIPTURE.
    a) We never interpret the unclear with the clear.
    b) We never with a single verse reverse an established theme developed by a larger number of verses.
    c) It is within the confines of clear and established doctrinal themes that we interpret those passages which seem difficult.
    d) It is not left to us to mystically or devotionally explain Scripture, but instead all doctrines are clearly established and given to us in the Word.

18. Give the key thought of these two passages as it pertains to this study. Deuteronomy 30:11-14; II Timothy 2:15.

CHAPTER 10

PERSONAL

NOTES

CHAPTER 11

DEALING WITH

DIFFICULT SCRIPTURE – PART III

In this chapter we will be using passages from the book of Acts. But first, it will be of value to deal with the Baptism of Jesus Christ as recorded in Matthew 3:13-17, Mark 1:9-11, Luke 3:21,22 and John 1:31-34. Because of the mystical appearance of the Holy Spirit at this time "descending as a dove" and "coming upon Him (Christ)" the baptism of Jesus is often given as evidence of the first historical record of the phenomenon referred to as the baptism and filling of the Holy Ghost. In this chapter we will establish that our studies are limited to the book of Acts for narrative examples of this phenomenon.

1. Read Luke 1:34,35

    a) How is Mary to conceive?

    b) What was the agent of this conception?

    c) What two descriptive phrases are used to describe the offspring?

2. Compare this with Christ's cousin, John the Baptist's experience with the Holy Spirit by reading Luke 1:13-15; 23-25.

    a) How was Elizabeth to conceive?

    b) Who was the agent of this conception?

c) Describe John the Baptist's relationship with the Holy Spirit (e.g. when did he receive the Holy Spirit?)

3. Describe the difference of spiritual states in terms of one's relationship with God and particularly the Holy Spirit between being "conceived of the Holy Spirit" (Jesus Christ) and "filled with the Holy Spirit while yet in his mother's womb" (John).

4. Read Luke 1:42-45

    a) What does Elizabeth do to the baby in Mary's womb? [Hint: The spiritual act usually reserved for God]

    b) How does Elizabeth describe the baby in verse 43?

    c) What is Elizabeth talking about in verse 45?

    d) In then, the baby, while in Mary's womb was indeed Christ, Lord and God, what was the baby's relationship with the Holy Spirit? Base this answer upon the sections on the Nature of God that you previously studied.

5. Read Luke 2:46-50

    a) When does this event occur in relationship to Jesus' baptism?

b) How does Jesus manifest His deity?

c) How does Jesus lay claim to His deity?

d) What must be the relationship of Jesus to the Holy Spirit at this point?

e) If Jesus did not have the fullness of the Holy Spirit or if He was in need of it, what would that have said about the relative spiritual state of John the Baptist and Jesus at this point? See Luke 1:15.

f) If Jesus did not have the fullness of the Holy Spirit, (e.g. 100% co-existence, relationship and knowledge) what would that have said about

His Deity

His sinlessness

6.   Read Luke 3:21,22

a) Does this passage say that Jesus was baptized with water?

b) Does it also say He was baptized with the Holy Spirit?

c) Does the passage say that Jesus was filled with the Holy Spirit?

d) Read Matthew 3:16, Mark 1:10, John 1:33. Do any of these passages make either of these claims?

7. How is the Trinity manifested in Jesus' baptism?

8. Why do you think God had the Holy Spirit manifest Himself in this way?

9. If Jesus was God and one with the Holy Spirit already, what is the meaning of this passage?

10. Having established that Jesus' baptism is not to be included in those passages dealing with the New Testament manifestation of the baptism of the Holy Spirit, we will now look at the phenomenon as related to us in the book of Acts.

    Complete the following table by reading the appropriate narrative passages and filling the appropriate data. The passages represent all historical narrative passages dealing with the baptism of and filling of the Holy Spirit in the book of Acts.

    In coming to any conclusions from these narrative passages, problems immediately unfold. Answer the questions 11 – 16 fully, giving reasons, examples, and proof texts from the table.

Passage	Timing & Setting	Method of receiving the Holy Spirit	Role of Church Leadership	Manifestation of the Spirit	People's desire
John 20:19-22					
Acts 2:1-13					
Acts 4:23-31					
Acts 8:14-18					
Acts 9:1-19					
Acts 10:44-48					
Acts 13:44-52					
Acts 19:1-7					

11. First, the method of receiving this baptism or filling is important. Are these passages helpful in our coming to a conclusion as to the method?

12. Second, the setting (e.g. timing of the experience) is important. Are these passages helpful in our coming to conclusions on when we are to be baptized?

13. Third, the role of church leadership is important. Are these passages helpful in our coming to any conclusions on this issue?

14. Fourth, the manifestations of the Holy Spirit's coming are important. Are these passages helpful in our coming to any conclusions on this issue?

15. Fifth, the desire for an awareness of the Holy Spirit is important. Were the people seeking the baptism of filling when it occurred? Are these passages helpful in coming to conclusions on this issue?

16. What conclusions can you draw concerning the value of the narratives in Acts for the establishment of a doctrine of universal value concerning the baptism and filling of the Holy Spirit?

17. The next table is significant in that it deals with the issue of salvation and the manifestation of the Holy Spirit. If there is a need to receive a baptism or filling or second grace experience, it can be assumed that this would be taught uniformly by the early church fathers' to converts. By filling in the table, observations concerning this can be drawn.

Passage	Explanation of Narrative	Were people saved? Who?	Manifestation of the Spirit
Acts 3:11-4:4			
Acts 8:25-40			
Acts 13:15-43			
Acts 13:44-49			
Acts 16:14,15			
Acts 16:22-40			
Acts 17:16-34			
Acts 18:1-5			

18. What has been determined about narrative Scripture and the doctrine of the Holy Spirit?

19. What has been determined about narrative Scripture in its relationship to doctrinal Scripture on the subject of the Holy Spirit?

20. What has been determined about the seeking of the baptism and/or filling of the Holy Spirit from narrative passages?

21. Give examples of people who the Bible says were actively seeking the baptism of the Holy Spirit (must be specifically stated).

22. From the table dealing with the receiving of the Holy Spirit, when was the last such manifestation?

    Scripture reference:_____

    Place:_____   Date:_____

    a) In the book of Ephesians, Paul instructs these very people on the doctrine of the Holy Spirit. When was this book written? Date:_____

    b) The earliest written doctrinal statement concerning the Holy Spirit's relationship with salvation occurs in the book of I Corinthians. When was this book written? Date: _____

c) Read Ephesians 1:13,14 and II Corinthians 1:21,22. What according to these passages is the Biblical doctrine of the baptism, receiving of the Holy Spirit?

23. Since these passages were written after Acts 19 and since there are no spiritual phenomenon as it pertains to the Holy Spirit and salvation recorded after Acts 19 and the writing of these passages, what conclusions can be drawn about the workings of the Holy Spirit?

Before these doctrines were laid down?

After these doctrines were laid down?

24. Which passages now shape our relationship with the Holy Spirit – the pre-doctrine narrative accounts or the post-doctrine doctrinal accounts? Why?

25. Of what value are these pre-doctrinal passages to us?

26. In your own words, summarize your understanding of the narrative passages in Acts as they pertain to the doctrine of the baptism and filling of the Holy Spirit.

CHAPTER 11

PERSONAL

NOTES

CHAPTER 12

SPEAKING IN

TONGUES

Speaking in tongues is perhaps the most controversial topic related to the Holy Spirit and many churches avoid teaching about it. While speaking in tongues in itself is not an issue, its association with being baptized or filled with the Holy Spirit has always been very controversial. Whether it is because of lack of knowledge or fear of losing the congregation, pastors are afraid to either support it or reject it. In this chapter we will study the Biblical principles of when and how it is appropriate to speak in tongues and if it is indeed a required manifestation of the Holy Spirit's presence in the life of a believer. Consider some statements made by influential people of the Pentecostal and Charismatic movements.

In his autobiography, David DuPlesis (known as Mr. Pentecost), said God showed him that tongues was a means for determining the divine will. "… the light clicked on. I was speaking to God in tongues, and He was speaking back to me in my mind. I began to find beautiful revelation that way. ... Praying in tongues proved to be a wonderful step in working my way out of such an impasse [in not being able to discern God's will]. I would merely pray in tongues, and if the idea held firm, then I knew it was real" (A Man Called Mr. Pentecost, pp. 76-78).

"God took the baptism in the Holy Spirit out of the theoretical by giving the believer an undeniable physical evidence when the believer was filled. That evidence is speaking with other tongues. ... The fact is those who receive the gift of the Holy Spirit will speak in tongues" (Charles Crabtree, "How Practical Is the Pentecostal Lifestyle?", Questions and Answers about the Holy Spirit, 2001, p. 70; Crabtree was assistant general superintendent of the Assemblies of God for 14 years.

Reference: http://www.wayoflife.org/database/pentecostaltongues.html

First, there are details about speaking in tongues that we cannot understand today. The type of speaking in tongues as was witnessed at the original Pentecost has not been witnessed again in over 2000 years.

1. The First Mention of Tongues

   a) Read Acts 2:6-11 and write down the appropriate phrase dealing with language(s) and/or tongue(s).

   Acts 2:6_____

   Acts 2:8_____

   Acts 2:11_____

   b) List below the various nations from which devout Jews were in Jerusalem at the time of Pentecost.

   c) What kind of "tongues" is this passage dealing about?

   d) Look up the Greek word for "tongues"

   e) Did the apostles know how to speak this language prior to the Pentecost?

   f) Who gave them the power to speak in a language that they had never learned before?

   g) Is "Tongues" in Acts 2 a mystic unknown language or a real earthly language?

2. The Private Prayer Language
   Speaking in tongues has become rare in public but continues to

be a vital expression of prayer in private. Many believe that this type of "tongues" is a "prayer language" – a way of communicating more effectively with God. They claim that this experience of praying in a private language gives them some kind of a special relationship with God that others don't have. They call this personal edification.

a) I Cor 14:4 Who is edified when one speaks in tongues? The speaker or the listener?

b) I Cor 14:10 What does every tongue/language have?

c) I Cor 14:6 Can anyone be edified by a tongue/language that is not understood?

d) I Cor 14:13 What should a person speaking in tongues pray for?

e) I Cor 14:19 What would Paul rather speak when he is in church?

f) Do you see any difference in "tongues" mentioned in Acts 2 and I Cor 14?

g) What do "tongues" mentioned in Acts 2 and I Cor 14 refer to?

h) I Cor 14:22 Tongues (or languages) are a sign for who?

i) I Cor 14:28 Can one speak to himself and God in a tongue/language that he/she cannot understand?

j) Do you see any example of believers or apostles speaking a "private prayer language"

k) What conclusion can you come to regarding the private prayer language doctrine?

The fact is that biblical tongues were real earthly languages that the Holy Spirit used as a sign for unbelieving Israel that the gospel is extended to all nations. This speaking in tongues is a fulfillment of Isaiah 28:11 where the prophet was speaking to the Jewish nation. Every time we see the gift of speaking in tongues exercised in Acts, Jews were present. In Acts 22, everything was going well as Paul, now a prisoner, was giving his defense until he mentioned the word "Gentiles" in verse 21. The crowd, consisting of Jews, could not accept that their Jewish God could also be the God of every man and every tongue.

3. Why tongues at Pentecost?

a) What does Phil 2:11 have to say about tongues?

b) What does Isaiah 28:11 have to say about tongues?

c) What relationship do you see between Isaiah 28:11 and the tongues at Pentecost in Acts and Phil 2:11?

Every believer, no matter what language he/she speaks will confess in their own language that Jesus is their Savior.

4. Biblical rules for speaking in tongues

   a) I Cor 14:20-22 Are tongues a sign for believers or unbelievers?

   b) In the context of Pentecostal-Charismatic movement, tongues are commonly used as a sign for being "baptized" or "filled" with the Holy Spirit. Do tongues have a place in today's church whose primary role is to prepare believers for the return of Christ? Explain.

   c) According to I Cor 14:2, who does the one speaking in tongues speak to?

   d) In I Cor 14:2, what does "mysteries" refer to? Is it a mysterious heavenly language? Relate this to speaking in tongues at Pentecost. Then relate this to today's church setting.

   Pentecost:

   Today's church:

   e) What are two gifts of the Holy Spirit related to tongues in I Cor 12:8-10

f) In church, what must accompany speaking in tongues? I Cor 14:27-28. Explain why.

g) How many people can simultaneously speak in tongues? I Cor 14:27? Explain in detail.

h) Can there be any vagueness, disorder or mysticism associated with speaking in tongues? I Cor 14:23,33

i) Can women speak in tongues in church?

I Cor 14:34-35

I Tim 2:11,12

j) Does Paul forbid speaking in tongues? I Cor 14:39

k) Are we bound to comply with Paul's teaching on speaking in tongues? I Cor 14:37. Why?

l) Write your own conclusion about a person who claims to speak in tongues by the Spirt and disobeys these rules laid down by Paul in I Cor 14?

5. Do all believers need to speak in tongues?

    I Cor 12:7-10

    I Cor 12:28-30

6. Did Jesus speak in tongues as a supernatural gift of the Holy Spirit when He was baptized? Give Scripture text to defend your answer.

    Does the Bible record Jesus ever speaking in tongues as a supernatural gift of the Holy Spirit?

7. Whenever the Bible discusses "tongues", what can you conclude from your study in this chapter? Is it speaking of earthly languages or a mystical heavenly language? Explain in detail your answer.

8. Can demons counterfeit the gift of speaking in tongues? II Cor 11:14.

With this chapter we conclude the difficult portions dealing with the doctrine of the Holy Spirit. It is important to have this background of the Holy Spirit to establish the remaining doctrines relating to the Holy Spirit's work in the life of every believer.

I promise the remaining chapters will not be as difficult as these.

Let move on.

CHAPTER 12

PERSONAL

NOTES

CHAPTER 13

THE NAMES & TITLES

OF THE

HOLY SPIRIT

Throughout the Bible, the Holy Spirit is called or referred to by several names and titles. A basic knowledge of these would enhance our understanding of His role or function in the life of a believer.

For each scripture or set of scriptures write down the name or title given to the Holy Spirit.

1. _____

   II Peter 1:21

   Luke 12:12

2. _____

   John 14:16

   John 15:26

   John 16:7

3. _____

   John 16:7-11

4. _____

   II Corinthians 1:22

   Ephesians 1:13-14

5. _____

   Judges 6:34

   Judges 14:19

6. _____

   Romans 8:9-11

   1 Corinthians 2:14

   Ephesians 4:30

7. _____

   Romans 8:26

8. _____

   John 14:16,17

   John 16:13

   I Corinthians 2:12-16

9. _____

   Matthew 3:16

   II Corinthians 3:17

   I Peter 1:11

10. _____

   Romans 8:2

11. _____

   John 14:26

   I Corinthians 2:13

12. _____

   Romans 8:16

Hebrews 2:4

Hebrews 10:15

13. In Isaiah 11:2 the Holy Spirit is described in 7 unique ways. List each of them and describe your understanding of what that means.

a) Spirit of _____

b) Spirit of _____

c) Spirit of _____

d) Spirit of _____

e) Spirit of _____

f) Spirit of _____

g) Spirit of _____

CHAPTER 13

PERSONAL

NOTES

CHAPTER 14

THE BAPTISM

AND FILLING

OF THE

HOLY SPIRIT

In Acts 2, we see the powerful and extraordinary entrance of the Holy Spirit as He for the first time came to indwell in a believer's life. A distinct difference in the work of the Holy Spirit between the Old Testament and the New Testament is the indwelling nature of the Holy Spirit. In the Old Testament the Spirit would come and go from the Saints empowering them for God's work but He did not indwell in their lives. In Judges 15:14 we see the Spirit come upon Samson giving him supernatural power to single handedly kill a thousand men. There are many other examples of this nature. But in the New Testament, Jesus reveals to His disciples the indwelling nature of the Spirit as we see in John 14:17. In this Chapter we will study the indwelling nature of the Holy Spirit and the doctrine of being "Baptized in the Spirit" and "Being Filled with the Spirit".

1. Read the following Scriptures and write down the New Testament relationship described between the Holy Spirit and the believer.

   a) John 14:17

   b) I Corinthians 6:19-20

   c) Ephesians 1:13-14

2. Read the following Scriptures and write down the life changing results of the Holy Spirit indwelling in a believer.

a) Titus 3:5, John 3:1-8

b) Romans 8:15-17

c) I Corinthians 12:13

d) I Corinthians 12:7-11

e) I Corinthians 2:12

f) Romans 8:26-27

g) Galatians 5:16, Romans 8:14

h) Galatians 5:22-23

i) Ephesians 4:30, I John 1:9

j) Ephesians 1:13-14

3. What role does the Holy Spirit play in the believer's life to accomplish II Corinthians 5:17?

4. Without doing any research on the topic, what is your understanding of the "Baptism of the Holy Spirit"?

5. Read the following scriptures and write down the future event described.

   a) Mark 1:8

   b) Acts 1:5

6. When was the future event in question 5 fulfilled? And what happened during this event? Acts 2:1-4

7. Read I Corinthians 12:12-13.

   a) Who are baptized into one body?

   b) Who baptizes new believers?

   c) What have new believers been given to drink(indwelling)?

8. When do believers become part of the "one body"?

   Romans 6:3-4

II Corinthians 5:17

9. Based on the study so far, what event does "Baptism of the Holy Spirit" refer to?

10. Now write your understanding of the "Baptism of the Holy Spirit"

11. Read John 14:16

    a) How much of the Holy Spirit indwells a believer at salvation?

    b) Does a believer need any more of the Holy Spirit after being born again?

    c) Does every believer receive the same indwelling of the Holy Spirit at salvation?

12. Without doing any research, write down your understanding of "Being filled with the Spirit".

13. Read the following scriptures and write down the condition of receiving the Holy Spirit.

    a) Gal 3:2

b) Gal 3:5

c) Gal 3:14

14. Does the believer have to earn more of the Holy Spirit to be filled with the Holy Spirit? Why or Why not?

15. Read the following scriptures and write down the irreversible event described.

a) Ephesians 1:13

b) II Corinthians 1:22

c) What does this mean in regards to the "filling of the Holy Spirit"? Did we not receive him completely at the time of salvation?

16. Read Ephesians 5:18. What are the two being contrast in this verse?

a)

b)

17. When a person is drunk with wine, what is now in control of the persons actions and behavior?

18. In contract, who is in control of a person who is filled with the Holy Spirit?

19. In Romans 8:9, what controlled our actions and behavior before we were baptized by the Holy Spirit?

    Who is or should be in control of our actions and behavior after we were baptized by the Holy Spirit?

20. Read the following Scriptures and write down what causes a believer to be outside of the control of the Holy Spirit.

    a) Ephesians 4:30

    b) I Thessalonians 5:19

    c) Does the believer have an option of being controlled by the Spirit or not? Explain why or why not.

    d) Does the Holy Spirit force a changed lifestyle on a believer?

21. Based on the study so far, write down your understanding of "Being filled with the Holy Spirit".

22. Read Romans 6:11-14. Write down a believer's responsibility in terms of expected to do and expected to not do.

    Expected to do

    Expected to not do

23. Read Galatians 5:16-26.

    How can a believer be assured that he/she will not give in to sinful desires?

    List all the action phrases that have the word Spirit in the phrase.

    a) Vs 16

    b) Vs 18

c) Vs 25

d) What is the result of following these action phrases? Vs 22, Rom 8:14

24. What do you now understand about "Walking in the Holy Spirit"?

25. Develop a relationship between "Baptized by the Holy Spirit", "Filled with the Holy Spirit" and "Walking with the Holy Spirit". Provide scripture references to prove your relationship.

CHAPTER 14

PERSONAL

NOTES

CHAPTER 15

THE POWER

OF THE

HOLY SPIRIT

Every believer is promised the supernatural power of being victorious over sin. It is not just being born again that is exciting, but it is being able to say no to sin when Satan comes knocking at your heart. In this act of refusing to sin, no matter how intense the temptation is or how desiring the sin is, we start to see the supernatural power that enables every believer to come closer to the "image of God" that Adam and Eve were created in before their fall. Even though the Holy Spirit did not indwell in a person until after Christ ascended to heaven, we see Him and His power right from the creation.

1. Read the following Scriptures and write down the role of the Holy Spirit.

    Genesis 1:1-2

    Job 26:13

    I Cor 2:10

    Eph 2:22

    Zech 4:6

2. Read the following passages in the Old Testament and write down how the power of the Spirit was demonstrated through ordinary people.

    Judges 14:6

    Judges 14:19

    Judges 15:14-16

    I Samuel 16:13

3. Read the following passages in the New Testament and write down the impact of the Holy Spirit in Jesus' life.

    Isaiah 11:2

    Matthew 12:28

    Luke 4:1a

    Luke 4:1b

    Luke 4:14

    Luke 4:18

    Acts 10:38

    Note that it is the same Spirit that has been given to all believers. We must realize that Jesus, being fully human (Phil 2:6-8), was able to perform the miracles, preach the good news and live in obedience to the Father because He was empowered by the Holy Spirit. Jesus' life of obedience and faithfulness is an example of how we should live depending on the same resource of the Holy Spirit that He had.

4. Read John 15:26, John 16:13, John 14:16 and John 14:26 a few times to understand the meaning and impact of these passages. Now describe in your own words what the Holy Spirit does and how He operates.

5. According to I Cor 3:16, where is the Holy Spirit in relation to the believer? Explain in detail what that means.

6. Let's read Isaiah 11:2. This verse describes the 7-fold Spirit of God that rested on Jesus Christ empowering Him for a life of obedience and ministry. List each of the Spirit's characteristics below. Note that there is one standalone characteristic and three pairs of two characteristics.

a)_____

b)_____and_____

c)_____and_____

d)_____and_____

7. <u>The Spirit of the Lord</u>

Review John 14:15-16.

a) What is the direction given?

b) What is the condition (starts with if)?

c) Who is going to help us keep this command?

d) When will this help come to the believer?

e) How long will the helper stay with the believer?

f) Where does this helper come from (Isaiah 11:2)?

g) Explain how the impossibility of keeping God's commandments is now made possible?

8. The Spirit of Wisdom & Understanding

    a) What is the important virtue we are commanded to get for ourselves? Prov 4:7

    b) What are the two characteristics that distinguish God's people based on Deut 4:5,6. Write in your own words what these two words mean.

    c) What did Eve depend on to make her decision when presented with the option of eating the forbidden fruit? Genesis 3:6

    d) Why do you think Eve make the decision to eat the forbidden fruit?

    e) In deciding to eat the forbidden fruit, who did Eve obey and who did Eve disobey?

    f) Read Deut 4:5,6 again. Then read Joshua 1:8
       i) Explain how a believer gains understanding.

       ii) Explain how a believer gains wisdom.

g) In gaining wisdom and understanding, what role do the Scriptures play?

h) In gaining wisdom and understanding, what role does the Holy Spirit play?

i) From Isaiah 11:2 and Joshua 1:8, move the following words into the table to determine the process of how the Holy Spirit works when it comes to wisdom and understanding.

READ   MEDITATE   UNDERSTANDING   WISDOM

WHAT   WHY/HOW

Joshua 1:8	Isaiah 11:2	Holy Spirit teaches

Now fill in the blanks in the following sentence to translate the table into a paragraph using the words from the table.

When we _____ the Word of God, the Holy Spirit will give us the _____ to learn _____ GOD wants for our lives. When we _____ on the Word of God, the Holy Spirit will give us the _____ to learn _____ Godly choices are critical. We also learn _____ to practically apply our understanding to make Godly choices.

The Holy Spirit uses the _____ and His _____ ability to give us Godly wisdom and understanding.

9. The Spirit of Counsel & Power
    Read Hebrews 4:14-16

128

a) Who is our High Priest?

b) In what way is this High Priest similar to us?

c) How can this High Priest help us in our weaknesses?

d) Read John 14:15-17. Who is Jesus, our High Priest going to send us?

_____Helper

e) Read John 16:13-15. Whose characteristics will this Helper have?

f) Fill in the blanks using John 16:13-15

Everything that the _____ has belongs to _____.

The _____will take from _____and declare them

to _____.

g) Fill in the blanks.

All the counsel we need comes directly from _____

through the _____.

h) Today, what does the Holy Spirit utilize to give us the counsel from Jesus Christ?

i) What are we commanded to do with the counsel of the Holy Spirit? Eph 5:18

j) What does "be filled with the Spirit" mean?

k) How does the Holy Spirit influence our obedience to God's counsel? Zech 4:6

l) Read Acts 1:8. What does the Holy Spirit enable us to be?

m) Define the word "witness". You can use a dictionary if needed.

n) How do we fulfill this great command of being Christ's witnesses?

o) What role does the Holy Spirit play in our witness of Christ?

p) From Isaiah 11:2 and Joshua 1:8, move the following words into the table to determine the process of how the Holy Spirit works when it comes to counsel and power.

MEDITATE   DO COUNSEL   POWER

HOW APPLICATION(APPLY)

Joshua 1:8	Isaiah 11:2	Holy Spirit teaches

Now fill in the blanks in the following sentence to translate the table into a paragraph using the words from the table.

When we _____ on the Word of God, the Holy Spirit will _____ us on _____ to make the right choices in every aspect of our lives. When we make a commitment to _____ the Word of God, the Holy Spirit will give us the _____ to _____ what we have learned through _____.

10. The Spirit of Knowledge & Fear of God
Read Proverbs 9:10

a) What do we gain from knowing God?

b) What do we gain by fearing God?

c) Read Ephesians 3:17-19. Write down the steps needed to fully know who God is.

d) From the same scriptures, what can we expect to understand(comprehend)?

e) How does our knowledge of God play a role in our willingness to obey God?

f) What is the main character of God that motivates us to obey Him? Explain your answer.

g) Write down your understand of what "fear of God" means.

h) How does our fear of God play a role in our willingness to obey God? Explain in as much detail as you can.

i) List some ways we (can) fear God in our daily lives.

j) Read Ephesians 5:1 What does Paul command us to do?

k) List several ways that we can fulfill the command in Ephesians 5:1.

Hebrews 4:15

Matthew 4:1-10

Matthew 15:32

Ephesians 2:4-9

Mark 1:9-11

Mark 1:35

Luke 19:10

John 8:10-11

Luke 23:34

John 18:3-5

Luke 19:10

l) Read Ephesians 5:2. What is the common motivator for both Christ and us?

m) How the Holy Spirit enable us to fulfill the commandment in Ephesians 5:1.

n) What is the evidence that you are correctly imitating Christ? See Ephesians 5:22,23. Explain your answer in detail.

o) From Isaiah 11:2 and Joshua 1:8, move the following words into the table to determine the process of how the Holy Spirit works when it comes to knowledge and fear of God.

READ(ING)   DO   KNOWLEDGE   FEAR OF GOD

WHAT   APPLICATION(APPLY)

Joshua 1:8	Isaiah 11:2	Holy Spirit teaches

Now fill in the blanks in the following sentence to translate the table into a paragraph using the words from the table.

When we _____ the Word of God, the Holy Spirit will give us the _____ to learn _____ God wants for our lives. When we make a commitment to _____ the Word of God, the Holy Spirit will give us the _____ to diligently _____ what we have learned through _____ the Word of God.

135

The Holy Spirit – A Doctrinal Study

11. Read Romans 8:14. What qualifies believers to be called the sons of God?

12. In your own words, summarize what you have learned about being "led by the Spirit".

13. Do you see any difference between "filled with the Spirit" (Chapter 14) and "led by the Spirit"? Why or Why not?

136

14. How do you know you are "led" or "filled" by the Spirit? See John 3:8 and refer to earlier questions in this chapter.

Being led by the Holy Spirit does not happen without being driven by the Word of God according to Joshua 1:8. As we READ, MEDITATE and DO (obey) the Word of God, the Holy Spirit through His knowledge, wisdom, counsel, understanding, power and fear of the Lord will supernaturally bring about His fruit to blossom in your life.

As you READ the Word of God, the Holy Spirit enables us through KNOWLEDGE and UNDERSTANDING to clearly determine WHAT God requires of us.

As you MEDITATE on the Word of God, the Holy Spirit enables us through WISDOM and COUNSEL to clearly determine WHY we have to obey God and HOW we can practically apply it in our lives.

As you DO (obey) the Word of God, the Holy Spirit enables us through POWER and FEAR to successfully APPLY biblical principles in every aspect of our lives.

CHAPTER 15

PERSONAL

NOTES

CHAPTER 16

THE

HOLY SPIRIT

**

CONCLUSION

Let us now combine the tables in the previous chapter into a single table to understand the process by which the Holy Spirit transforms our lives utilizing the Word of God. Place the words in the appropriate cell.

READ   MEDITATE   DO

UNDERSTANDING   KNOWLEDGE

WISDOM   COUNSEL

POWER   FEAR OF THE LORD

WHAT   WHY/HOW   APPLICATION

Joshua 1:8	Isaiah 11:2	The Holy Spirit Teaches

You must let God's Word and the enablers of the Holy Spirit control every aspect of your life. You will then start to see a supernatural transformation happening in the very core of your heart.

Galatians 5 describes this transformation, but I do want to caution you that it does not happen overnight. Just because a sinner is born again does not necessarily mean that a switch is turned on and change happens. A switch is indeed turned on and the tiniest of sparks with a desire to change is fired up. This spark must be kept aflame so that the desire turns into a passion resulting in an uncompromising commitment to holiness.

Any change includes a previous and a new state. Read Galatians 5:19-23 and summarize the previous state and the new state described in this passage.

Previous State:

New State:

From a human change perspective we call this a paradigm shift. T. S. Kuhn, a philosopher of science, defined and popularized the concept of "paradigm shift" in 1962. He defines it as a radical change in underlying beliefs and in the way one thinks. It does not just happen, but is driven by agents of change. That is how the supernatural transformation happens in a Christian. Our way of thinking and acting must radically change from the *works of the flesh* to the *fruit of the Spirit*. This should be driven by the Holy Spirit utilizing the Word of God to transform our minds. Romans 12:1-2.

You see, before a person is born again, it is natural for a person to do what the flesh desires. Now that one is born again and has the Spirit indwelling in the heart, new believers have to be sensitive to the leading of the Spirit. What comes naturally must now be run past the Holy Spirit for a determination of whether that action is now acceptable to God or not. That is a dramatic change. No longer can one depend on feelings or emotions or logic or what makes sense.

The Holy Spirit now indwells in our lives as a reminder and a guarantee that a change is now possible and will occur if we are led by the Spirit. By submitting to the indwelling nature of the Holy Spirit, every Christian is given a chance to acquire wisdom, understanding, counsel, power, knowledge, and live in the fear of the Lord. It is only when a person submits to the Holy Spirit that he or she sees the powerful, life-changing impact of the Word of God. May God accomplish in you what He has started to do when He found you, saved you and adopted you into his family. Philippians 1:3-6.

Make sure you know your doctrines relating to the Baptism and Filling of the Holy Spirit. Don't fall into subtle traps the devil brings your way. Study the Word of God with the help of the Holy Spirit to establish sound Biblical doctrines. May the Holy Spirit empower you and transform you into Christ's image.

> Be diligent to present yourself approved to God, a worker who does not need to be ashamed, rightly dividing the truth. (II Timothy 2:15)

The grace of our Lord Jesus Christ be with you.

CHAPTER 16

PERSONAL

NOTES

PERSONAL

NOTES

PERSONAL

NOTES

PERSONAL

NOTES

PERSONAL

NOTES